In the Meantime

Hope, Healing, and Survival
for the Tired Heart

Also by Deedee Cummings

Books for Children:

Love Is…

Think of it Like This!

My Trip to the Beach

I Want to be a Bennett Belle

My Dad's Job

Heart

If A Caterpillar Can Fly, Why Can't I?

Like Rainwater

This is The Earth

In the Nick of Time

Kayla: A Modern-Day Princess

Kayla: A Modern-Day Princess—Dishes, Dancing, and Dreams

Kayla: A Modern-Day Princess—Tough as Tulle

Kayla: A Modern-Day Princess—These Shoes Are Made for Dancing

Kayla: A Modern-Day Princess—A Little Magic

Kayla: A Modern-Day Princess Activity Book

In the Nick of Time Too

Hope in the Nick of Time

Hope in the Nick of Time Activity Book

Books for Adults:

How to Dream

How to Dream Workbook

In the Meantime Workbook

In the Meantime

Hope, Healing, and Survival
for the Tired Heart

Deedee Cummings

www.makeawaymedia.com

"Every storm runs out of rain."

~Dr. Maya Angelou

Contents

PART I
NAMING THE PAIN

Chapter 1
The Fog We're Living In

There has always been a battle between good and evil.
Always has been.
Always will be.

We have been lulled into a sense of upward progress or mobility. Our country went from slavery and Jim Crow to milestones such as women's rights and civil rights, the Americans with Disabilities Act, the Affordable Healthcare Act and the Respect for Marriage Act. We wrongly assumed that our country was progressing, would continue to progress, and once a right was granted (or acknowledged) the right was here to stay.

We were wrong.

As a result, we became complacent. We felt secure in our rights, while others spent every waking hour scheming to snatch them back before we were finished celebrating the win.

And they did.

The retaking of a *right* has shocked us and left us in a fog. This is what I hear from my therapy clients, and it is how I feel too. If you have ever hit your head then you know that feeling: the ringing, the stupor, the cloud. And then comes the heaviness.

Some mornings, the heaviness wakes you before the sun does. It's the first thing you feel when you wake up. A presence of mind that there will be no possible way you can move yourself from your current spot.

Before your feet even hit the floor, the thoughts come. *What's happening to this country? What are we walking into today? What did they take away from us overnight while we were sleeping?*

You're not imagining it. You're not being dramatic. This is the fog we're living in. I hear about it daily. I feel it daily. It's real.

It's the fog of disorientation, the kind that creeps in slowly and then suddenly feels like it's everywhere, clouding your hope, your motivation, your joy. It's political. It's personal. It's emotional. It's spiritual. It's heavy.

And it's by design. I need you to remember this. The way you feel is a targeted approach to make you feel so defeated you quit before you even begin.

Do not let them win.

You Are Not the Problem

If you've been feeling numb, overwhelmed, angry, exhausted, or flat-out hopeless, I want to say this clearly:

There is nothing wrong with you.

You are having a very normal response to a very abnormal reality.

When policies pass that strip people of healthcare, that erase protections, that funnel resources to the few while silencing the urgent needs of the many, you feel it all over. You feel it in your chest, your stomach, your sleep patterns, your relationships, your thoughts, your hopes, and your dreams. Even if you don't know exactly what's happening, you know something is happening.

You're a human being. You care. That is not weakness. That is wisdom. That is strength, even though you feel defeated.

This hurts. You might wonder why it feels so personal, so sharp. Maybe you ask yourself, *why does this hit me harder than it seems to hit other people?* Because it *is* personal.

When people in power ignore suffering—or worse, create more of it—it sends a message that your life doesn't matter as much as others.

If you're a woman, a person of color, LGBTQIA+, have different abilities, are poor, or part of any historically marginalized group, you've already spent much of your life fighting to be seen. And now, when progress feels like it's slipping through our fingers, it's not just political. It's existential.

We're not just grieving policies.
We're grieving possibility.

That fog you feel around you is despair. Despair is the complete loss or absence of hope.

Despair is a tool. It is the very thing used by people in power to convince you to give up. Despair says:

- *You're too small to matter.*
- *Nothing will change.*

- *Why even try?*

But that is not the truth.

That's the **weaponized version of hopelessness.** The kind that keeps us from organizing, dreaming, voting, creating, daring, hoping, and caring. The kind that convinces us to check out when what we really need is to check in—with ourselves and with each other.

Despair thrives in disconnection.

That's why this book exists.
We will not live in despair.
We will not allow ourselves to be disconnected.

We Begin by Naming It

We begin our journey together by telling the truth.

This is a hard time. A heavy time. A confusing, chaotic, aching, hurtful, painful time. It hurts to know that so many people seem so unbelievably cruel. It hurts even more to learn that some of these people are our friends, neighbors, coworkers, church members, and even our own relatives. This realization has offered us a double whammy as we try to resurface from the fog and ask ourselves how the virus of hate, selfishness, or indifference spread to people we thought we knew.

Naming the fog helps us cut through it. Once we know what we're facing, we can decide what to do next.

Take a deep breath here.
All the way in.
All the way out.
Pause.
We don't need to have it all figured out.
We just need to remember one thing:
The fog doesn't last forever. And even if you can't see the path, the path *is* there.

It *is* there.

Despair is their tool.
Hope is ours.
Love never fails.

***

Reflection prompts

1. What has been weighing most heavily on your heart lately?

2. What part of you feels hardest to carry right now?

   Give it a name. Speak to it with compassion instead of judgment. Let it know it's allowed to be here, but it is *not* all of you.

3. Write a list of three things you wish someone would say to you right now. Now, say them to yourself—out loud. These are powerful words that are speaking to you through you. Make sure you are taking full and complete breath cycles as you read what you have written out loud.

4. When has love shown up for you in a time of fear or despair—no matter how small? Let yourself remember that moment. Let it remind you that love still lives inside people.

5. What does "love winning" look like in your life? Not in a poetic sense, but in your real, ordinary world. Describe what it might feel like, sound like, or create around you.

Chapter 2
When Leaders Don't Lead

There's a specific kind of heartbreak that comes from watching people in power make decisions that hurt the very people they were elected to protect. It feels like a betrayal.

Because that's exactly what it is.

We were all raised to believe that leadership means service. That elected officials represent the will of the people. That *public servants* serve the *public*.

What happens when we are confronted with the fact that this is not the case? What happens when we look around and realize the people with the most power seem to care the least?

Disconnect becomes outright disrespect. Look at their voting patterns. They are telling you how they feel about you every time they vote. It's not just the bills they pass or the ones they block. It's the smugness. Going on social media and gaslighting you by telling you that their vote did not matter that much because we are all going to die one day.

It's also in the silence. Ducking out of the halls to escape reporters, then later taking a photo where they are in front of an impromptu correctional structure built to house misery.

Believe your eyes, not the explanation. This is real. *Yes, people really can be this heartless.*

When leaders don't lead with empathy, people stop feeling safe. They stop feeling seen. And worst of all, they start to believe their pain doesn't matter.

Now look at your voting patterns. That is how *you* tell them how you feel about *them*.

We are in control when we vote.

Your pain matters. Your life matters. Your voice matters. Even when the people in power pretend otherwise.

This Is Not Our Fault

There is only one group of people to blame and those are the people who are spending their days planning how to take advantage of everyone else. This is *their* fault, but it is in *our* control. When things fall apart at the top, it's easy to internalize the chaos at the bottom.

You may find yourself wondering:

- *Did I not do enough?*
- *Did my vote not count?*
- *What more could I have done?*

But this isn't about blame. It's about power, and how it gets hoarded, manipulated, and wielded to protect the powerful. This isn't your fault. It never was.

You were never meant to carry the entire weight of a nation on your back. But here you are, shouldering the consequences of leadership failure.

I see you.
I see your grief, your rage, your disillusionment.

But I also see your strength.
Your refusal to look away.
Your heartbreak is a signal of your humanity.

Your heartbreak is a gift because it means you care. It also means you're not an asshole. Take comfort in that. Wear your good human badge like the honor it is!

It's tempting to shut down. It is so tempting to let their apathy become your apathy. In so many ways it feels like life would be easier if you could just somehow train yourself not to care.

To say: *If they don't care, why should I?*

But that's what they're hoping for—that you'll tune out, grow numb, give up.

I am asking you: please, do not let them win. Your ability to care in a time designed to make you indifferent is *revolutionary* all by itself. It's spiritual. It's necessary.

Yes, we are tired.
Yes, we are allowed to rest.
But we cannot let their apathy infect our hope.
We cannot sit back and allow their apathy to become our despair.

If we stop hoping, we stop dreaming.
If we stop dreaming, we stop fighting.
If we stop fighting, we stop building.
And if we stop building, we never get the future we deserve.

The Good News About Bad Leaders

Here's what they don't want you to know:

Bad leadership doesn't erase your power. It just makes your power harder to see. But it's still there. Your influence still matters in your home, your neighborhood, your community, your vote, your art, your words, your kindness, and your boundaries.

We don't need perfect leaders to create powerful change. We just need people—people like you— who refuse to stop believing in something better. Throughout history, there have always been leaders who rose to power not to serve, but to dominate. Not to build, but to hoard. Not to protect life, but to consolidate control.

These "leaders" have always used weapons of fear, hate, disinformation, nationalism, racism, greed, and manufactured division to fuel their rise. They have always found a way to make cruelty sound like common sense. They have always twisted laws to benefit themselves while somehow convincing a group of people they were actually being protected.

And it works. For a while.

The people grow tired. Divided. Distracted.
The systems buckle. The freedoms shrink. The fog thickens.

But here's what history shows us over and over again:

Selfish power is never sustainable.
And unjust rulers never last.

Movements Rise. Empires Fall. Always.

From pharaohs to fascists, from colonizers to corrupt kings—those who try to seize power through fear, cruelty, or unchecked ego are always met with resistance.

Sometimes slowly.
Sometimes from within.
Sometimes by the very people they underestimated.

But it always comes.

It always comes because people can only be lied to for so long. Truth only stays buried for so long. And fear can only win *for so long* until someone remembers their power and starts using it.

This is tough for me to admit here, but I am going to tell the story anyway because I hope it helps someone else.

I believe in God. I love God. I'm just gonna state that right up front. *However*, right after the 2024 election I was physically and mentally ill. I was sick. *As a dog.* Very little could console me. What I felt was fear and disgust. But I also felt rage that so many people I knew could have voted for someone who campaigned on the fact that they would hurt me and the people I loved. People voted for that. That *hurt*.

All over social media there were comments everywhere of people expressing fear and people replying with, "God is in control." These words did not comfort me. At all. I found myself thinking, "Yeah well, God was in control during slavery and the Holocaust too."

I'm being brutally honest with you here. I am sharing a feeling and a thought process that was not pleasant, but it was real. Then I felt an additional layer of shame and guilt from having these feelings.

I felt ungrateful to the God I believe in.

So I called my mother-in-law, now in her 70s. A woman who actually saw signs that said "Whites only" with her own eyes. A woman who was alive as a young adult during the civil rights movement at the same time Dr. Martin Luther King Jr. was alive. A woman who *absolutely* loves the Lord.

And I said, "Please don't think badly of me, but I need help with this 'God is in control' concept." And I told her why these words brought me zero comfort in that moment.

And she gave me four words I will hold on to for the rest of my life: "*Things must be revealed.*"

These words not only brought me comfort. I *believe* God is in control.

This is why it is so important and so healthy to talk about your feelings.

Platitudes—even spiritual ones—can feel hollow when pain is deep and injustice is unchecked. My mother-in-law's words offer a grounded theology of truth-telling, clarity, and divine accountability.

"Things must be revealed" is not an excuse or a dismissal. It's not a way of saying, "Let bad things happen because God will fix it later." It's a truth about transformation, and history, and what we can count on as a collective spirit.

**Hate can't be dismantled until it's exposed.
Injustice can't be overturned until it's named.
Corruption can't be stopped until it's undeniable.**

Your pain, your discomfort, your disillusionment—none of it is faithless. It's *evidence that you are awake.*

That your spirit refuses to make peace with lies.

And maybe what "God is in control" means isn't that suffering is approved or ordained. Maybe it means that *even in the suffering,* truth will rise. Even in the chaos, exposure is happening. Even when it feels like the world is on fire, the masks are falling off.

What's hidden must come to light.
What's rotten must be uncovered.
And what's broken must be seen before it can be rebuilt.

That is not the absence of God.
That is the work of God.

I am so grateful for this one conversation, as it completely changed my entire perspective, and I have not been sick one day since.

Now, I know some of you do not believe in God, which is your right, and I am absolutely not here to proselytize. Even if you do not believe in a God, I want you to hang on to these powerful words from a wise woman named Therese Pettaway who was born in Silver City, Mississippi in 1951.

Things must be revealed.

This truth still holds whether you believe in a God or not.

We Are the Continuation of Every Uprising

We come from people who have:

- Escaped dictatorships

- Overthrown tyrants

- Resisted slavery, genocide, apartheid, and surveillance

- Dismantled empires

- Marched, organized, published, voted, and fought for their very existence

My mother, Andrea Mast Pecchioni, was born in Nacogdoches, Texas, in 1945. My husband's mother, Therese Stokes Pettaway, was born in 1951. In their childhood they could not drink out of a water fountain in a public courthouse. Their generation, now in their 70s, *are living proof that oppressive power never gets the last word.*

If it did, I wouldn't be here. And you would not be here with me now reading this book.

We are the fruit of resistance.
The descendants of courage.
The answer to someone else's prayer for justice.

When It Feels Like Evil Is Winning—Zoom Out

Evil leaders do rise. But they also *always fall.*

Their grip tightens when people forget they have a say, but the moment we remember our voice, our vote, our vision, they start to self-destruct.

Catch yourself when you find yourself thinking "it's over." It's not.

No one holds power forever.
Especially those who abuse it.

That's not optimism.
That's *history.*

***

Reflection Prompts:

1. When was a time when you felt truly seen by a political or policy leader? What did that feel like?

2. How has leadership disappointment shaped your views on power?

3. What leadership qualities do you admire, and how do you embody them in your own life?

4. What would you say to a friend who is feeling completely disillusioned right now? Write this message on an index card and place it somewhere where you will stumble across it (like your wallet or coat pocket).

5. What helps you demonstrate that you care without becoming consumed by the constant barrage of negativity in the media?

Chapter 3
It's Not You, It's Grief

There's a quiet mourning happening across the country. Truthfully, there is a mourning happening across the world.

You feel it in the silence after the news plays. You feel it when you scroll past another heartbreaking headline. You feel it with the announcement of a bill passing or the Supreme Court issuing a ruling. You feel it when you lie awake at night, not sure if you're anxious, or pissed off, or just sad—or all three.

You might think you're burnt out, or just tired, or exceptionally irritable. But here's the truth no one is really saying:

You're grieving.

And you're not alone.

What We've Lost

Grief isn't always about death.
Grief is about loss. And right now, we're surrounded by it.

We're grieving:

- The illusion of stability

- Leaders who made us feel represented, or proud, or like we had leaders

- A sense of morality among us as a commonality

- Trust in systems we thought would protect us

- Healthcare access

- Safety in our schools and communities

- The belief that progress always moves forward

- Our rights

- Trust that the moral universe bends toward justice

- A vision of a future that once felt possible

We're grieving certainty. We're grieving hope. We're grieving the security of healthcare and a social safety net that might keep most of us from having to work till the day we die. We're grieving our future. We're grieving the dream of America as it *could have been.* Hell… as it *should have been.*

Even when you can't name it fully, your body knows. That tightness in your chest? That edge in your voice? That constant background fatigue?

All that's grief, too.

Grief Is Not a Sign of Weakness

We don't do a very good job of talking about grief in this country. Our culture gets so many things about grief wrong. You may think, b*ut I haven't lost as much as other people. I should be fine.*

No. Grief is not a competition. It is a human response to loss, and everyone has a right to feel it. This grief shows you that you still care. It proves your humanity hasn't been numbed. It tells you that your heart is still tender and awake. That, too, is a kind of power. As much as grief sucks, be grateful for it. It means that you are human. It means that some billionaire is spending hundreds of millions of dollars to run propaganda in an attempt to control your mind and your voice and it did not work on you.

Toni Morrison said, "No more apologies for a bleeding heart when the opposite is no heart at all. Danger of losing humanity must be met with more humanity."

Your grief is a bleeding heart. Your grief is more humanity. No apologies for that.

Grief Is Not Linear— And It's Not Quick

One day you may feel energized. Hopeful. Ready to fight. The next, you might feel like crawling under the covers and pretending the world doesn't exist. This is normal. You're not "slipping backwards." You're moving through waves.

That's how grief works—it comes in waves, not checklists. Grief requires compassion. *Especially* self-compassion. Another thing our culture gets all wrong.

Grieving While Living

Here's what makes this season so complex:
We're grieving *while* trying to survive.

While parenting.
While working.
While cleaning up after policies that break our communities.

While cleaning our clothes, the kitchen floor and the dishes.
While trying to stay sane in a world that keeps shifting under our feet.

Grieving while living is exhausting. But it's also sacred because it is purpose. It is the very reason we are here.

It's a reminder that your spirit hasn't given up.
You are still here. Still breathing. Still caring.

Even in grief, there is life.
There is hope.

You Don't Have to "Get Over It"—You Can Grow *With* It

We don't move on from grief. We move *with* it. We grow around it. We learn how to carry it with grace and grit. Grief can live beside joy. It can make room for action. It can even deepen our purpose.

Don't spend one minute of joy followed by regret or remorse. We are free. We have a right to experience joy. We *should* experience joy. Otherwise, what are we living for?

Your joy and your rage can both take up space in your day, in your mind, and in your heart.

The truth is: many of us are grieving a country we hoped to believe in. But that grief doesn't mean it's the end of the story.

Sometimes grief is what gives us the courage to write a new story.

***

Reflection Prompts:

1. What have you lost in the last few years that you haven't fully grieved?

1. How does your grief show up in your body?

2. What would it feel like to treat yourself with compassion instead of judgment?

3. What have you gained or discovered *because* of what you've lost?

4. What does healing *look like* to you right now?

PART II
FINDING SHELTER IN THE STORM

Chapter 4
Protecting Your Mental Health When the World Feels Unsafe

We were not built for constant crisis. We—you and I—were built for connection, creativity, and care. And yet, here we are, navigating a world that feels increasingly chaotic, unpredictable, and unsafe. Not just politically, but emotionally. Spiritually. Systemically. Existentially.

It's a lot.

And your nervous system knows it.

If you feel frayed, numb, on edge, or constantly alert, there is nothing wrong with you. That is your brain doing its best to protect you from harm. But here's the catch:

You still deserve peace. Even in a world like this.

You can still find peace. Even in a world like this.

You should take the time to create something. Especially in a world like this.

The Line Between Informed and Overwhelmed

There is a point at which staying informed becomes staying in a state of panic. We cannot possibly keep up with today's news cycle. And we should not try to.

You scroll to feel less helpless, and you end up feeling worse. You watch the news to feel aware, and it leaves you paralyzed. You absorb trauma, not realizing you're collecting it in your body like a sponge.

You are not obligated to carry the entire world.

Yes, we must care. But we must also **choose how we care.**

Because if you're not careful, the fire outside becomes a fire within.

This is a Propaganda Tactic

You should know that the flood of news stories happening every day is by design. Poor leaders often spread so much disinformation that you do not know what is real. We need to be careful where we get our news from. Even then, do not feel pressured to keep up with it all.

Personally, I watch one morning news show that I trust for twenty minutes. There is also one person who shares present day news, often in a historical context, almost every day on a social media platform. I read that one column. And then I am done. For the day.

I don't watch the 6 am, the 9 am, the noon, the 5 pm, the 5:30 pm, the 6 pm, the 10 pm, and the 11 pm news. But I know people who do.

I can't keep my TV on the news all day. When I go to get my tires rotated and the tire shop has a TV on the news in the lobby, I position myself where I will not even glance at that screen and I read a book or listen to a nurturing podcast.

I typically watch one show Monday through Friday for twenty minutes. There is also one person I trust who recaps major headlines every day on social media, and that is all the news I allow myself to absorb. That one person is a professor and historian named Heather Cox Richardson, and I believe she is a truth teller. These limits on news updates help me not feel as overwhelmed, so that I am able to move on with my day. I do not need to know much more than that because I cannot hang on to much more than that.

Regardless of how you get your news, consider both the source and the number of issues you are tracking. If you have questions or concerns about an issue, look for more information from credible sources on *only that one issue* and that is *the one issue* you tackle. That is the *one issue* you donate to. That is the *one issue* you call your representative about.

You cannot feel responsible for it all. I trust that I am handling my issue and you are handling yours. If we all handled one issue near and dear to us, then we have done our best for the day. This does not mean never donate to any other cause or never write a letter about any other issue. You just cannot live with the pressure to attend to every fire. I am watering *my* burning building. You have to water yours.

Your Mind Needs Shelter, Too

We talk about protecting our communities, our rights, our freedoms. But what about our minds? Mental health isn't a luxury. It's a survival strategy. You can't fight, dream, love, create, or rebuild if your mind is in a constant state of collapse.

Here's what no one tells you:

Tuning out sometimes is part of tuning in to your values.
Rest is a political act.
Guarding your joy is revolutionary.
Creating is revolutionary.
And turning off the noise doesn't mean you don't care. It means you care enough to stay well enough to keep going. Like the burning building, I trust that if I'm down a day, you're up. And when you're down for the day, I got us.

What You're Allowed to Do

You are allowed to:

- Stop doomscrolling. Please stop doomscrolling. Don't just put the phone down—put it out of your reach. Step away from the phone.

- Delete the app for a week. (Whatever your vice is.)

- Say out loud "I don't have the capacity for that right now."
- Cry over things that didn't happen to you directly.
- Let your laughter live beside your heartbreak.
- Feel joy without guilt.
- Stop and smell flowers, even knowing that pain is happening right now.
- Create beauty in the middle of a war.

You are allowed to turn toward what heals you.

Find Your Anchors

When the world is spinning, we need anchors—routines, people, rituals, spaces, even objects—that bring us back to ourselves and remind us why we are here. These could be:

- A quiet walk with your phone off
- Reading that book you've been putting off
- A favorite meal made with intention
- Playing with your child or your pet
- Journaling without judgment

- A playlist that steadies your breath
- Saying no *without* explanation
- Putting a puzzle together
- Breathing deep into your belly
- Finding and enjoying a quiet space
- Painting, not because you are good at it, but because it is fun
- Talking to someone who reminds you that you matter
- Laughing together at something too silly to explain
- Putting together a flower bouquet—*for yourself*
- Capturing beauty in a photo

These aren't extras.
These are tools of resistance.
They keep you rooted in your own humanity when the world forgets it.

Anchors will often look like joy. Anchors may look like the very thing we are fighting for. It's okay. Celebrate your anchors.

Your joy and your rage can coexist.

Do not experience a moment of guilt for experiencing joy. A life with no joy is not a life no matter what period in the timeline we are on.

Protecting Yourself Is Powering Up

There is a reason bad leaders want you to stay exhausted. Tired people are easier to manipulate. Easier to silence. Tired people start the day feeling defeated. Tired people give up more easily. Tired people do not dream, or hope, or build or create. But rest is resistance. Mental clarity is rebellion. And emotional regulation is strength.

Don't blow with the wind. Stay on your square. Don't clock on someone because you had the "right" to. It is rarely worth your energy.

Social media has grown out of control with trolls and bots who are planted purposefully to divide and exhaust us. Even if you know with certainty a comment was not made by a troll, learn to conserve your energy. Social media comments are not where this battle will be won.

Do you need another argument to stop arguing on social media? Take the words of my mother:

Never wrestle with a pig. You both get dirty, and the pig likes it.

We need to conserve our energy. Let ignorant comments stand on their own. Sit down somewhere and stop burning up my light bill as my grandmother would say. Get your footing and hold the line. Everyone does not deserve our attention and our energy.

Your health is part of the movement and that includes mental health. Take care of it like your life depends on it—because it does.

***

Reflection Prompts:

1. What does "safety" mean to you right now?

2. What's one boundary you could set this week to protect your peace?

3. How does your body react to stress? What helps it feel safe again?

4. What makes you feel grounded when the world feels like it's spinning?

5. What's one thing you can release today that you were never meant to carry?

Chapter 5
The Power of
Micro-Resistance

When the world feels like it's falling apart, the idea of making change can feel impossibly big. Too big.

You may ask:

- *Can one person really make a difference?*
- *Are we really signing another petition or calling another senator?*
- *Does any of it actually matter?*

And the answer is:

Yes. But not always in the ways you think. Change is often not dramatic. Even when it seems like it should be. It's usually not. Change is a ripple. And you are a crucial ring in that ripple. Hold on to that.

Small Acts Keep the Fire Burning

Not every act of resistance is loud. Not every change happens on a stage. Sometimes the most revolutionary thing you can do is refuse to go numb.

That's *micro-resistance.*

It's the quiet, daily choices that say:

"I will not let the world make me indifferent."
"I may be one person, but I still matter."
"I am still in control of *me.*"
"I will not hand over my hope."

Protect your hope at all costs. *That* is resistance. *That* is revolutionary. If you cannot do anything but hold on to your hope, I want you to know you are doing a lot.

You don't have to flip an entire system overnight. But you *can* keep *your* light from being put out. *That* is power. They cannot control you. They cannot stop you. They cannot hold you. This little light of mine….

Micro-Resistance Looks Like This:

- Instead of doomscrolling, try hopescrolling for grassroots organizations to donate money too. Even if it is just $5.

- Calling a local rep on your lunch break

- Putting a banned book in a Little Free Library

- Refusing to laugh at that cruel joke at work

- Correcting misinformation—~~kindly but~~ firmly

- Creating art that challenges the status quo

- Telling your story

- Helping someone make their choice easier and safer to make

- Making your own family safer, freer, more aware, more honest

- Write a letter of hope to a friend who needs the reminder

- Telling someone, "You're not alone"

- Watching, videoing, standing

These are *small*, yes. But they are not *insignificant*.

These are ripples.
They create cracks in the foundation.
And over time, cracks change everything.
So, when you think what you are doing is not enough, remember this…

We Don't Need Heroics.We Need Consistency

It's not about one viral moment. It's about a thousand tiny moments that seem to go unseen.

The civil rights movement wasn't built in a day. It was built in kitchens and church basements, at lunch counters, living rooms, and library steps. It was built on songs and pamphlets and handshakes and people choosing to care, day after day. That's how we build now, too. Not with perfection. With presence.

This is why it matters that you are rested and in control of your mind and your reactions.

Resting is refueling.

Your Life *Is* the Movement

You don't have to be an organizer to be part of the work.

Maybe your resistance is teaching your children about injustice in age-appropriate ways.
Maybe it's protecting your rest.
Maybe it's starting a conversation no one else wants to have.
Or volunteering in a food pantry.
Giving books to kids.
Reading books to kids.
Sending thank you notes to those who are speaking up when you, for whatever reason, cannot.

In 2020 during the Black Lives Matter movement in the wake of the murders of Breonna Taylor and George Floyd, I was busy more than twelve hours a day seeing therapy clients. I desperately wanted to go to the marches and protests that were being held right downtown in my hometown of Louisville, Kentucky. We were in a full-blown one-hundred-year pandemic and trauma (both racial and medical) had vicariously passed to me in loads.

As a mental health therapist, I did not have the energy to protest, but I greatly admired local poet Hannah Drake, who perfectly said everything my heart felt.

I followed her on social media and liked everything she posted as a way to show support for her message to the world.

One day she posted that her feet hurt from protesting, and she had worn out her tennis shoes. So, what did I do? I mailed her a pair of new tennis shoes so she could keep marching when I could not. I believed the thought would buoy not only her feet, but her heart, as well. Small actions add up. We cannot all be on the frontline. We do not all have to be.

Micro-resistance says:
I will not hand my spirit over to injustice.

Even when I'm tired. Especially if I'm tired.

You are not alone in this.
Every act of care is part of the storm that clears the way for something new.

***

Reflection Prompts:

1. What's one small action I can take today that aligns with my values?

2. When was the last time I made a difference in someone's life (even in a small way)?

3. What parts of my day could become acts of resistance?

4. What injustice stirs something in me that I can no longer ignore?

5. How can I honor my limits *and* still show up?

Chapter 6
Sacred Ground— What You Can Still Control

When the world feels unstable, it's easy to start believing that *everything* is out of your hands.

And that is exactly how systems of oppression keep going—by convincing you that you have no power.

But you do.

Even in a world where so much has been taken, **there are still parts of your life that are sacred. Choices that are yours. Ground that belongs to you.**

This chapter is about reclaiming that ground.

You Still Own Your Breath

No matter what policies pass,
No matter who sits in the highest office,
No matter what gets banned or broken,
You still control your breath.

And your breath is a gateway. It grounds you in the now. It brings oxygen to the parts of you the world tries to suffocate. It reminds your nervous system: *I am here. I am safe enough in this moment to breathe.*

Your breath is yours.
Your breath is in your control.
Return to it. Often.

You Still Control Your Voice

You get to choose what you say.
You get to choose what you don't say.
How you speak to your children.
What you post online.
Who you challenge at a family gathering.
What truths you whisper to your own heart when no one's watching.

When leaders lie, when headlines gaslight, when fear takes over the conversation, **your voice becomes more important than ever.**

Let it be truthful. Let it be kind. Let it be bold. Let it be healing.
And let it be yours.

You Still Control What You Water

You've heard it said that where your attention goes, your energy follows.

But here's a new one: Only apply your energy where it is received.

Even in hard seasons, you get to choose:

- Which voices you amplify
- What stories you consume
- What kind of beauty you make room for
- Who gets your time, your kindness,
- Who gets your yes

This is sacred.

If no one has ever told you—if no one has ever given you permission—here it is:
It's okay to protect your peace.

It's okay to be intentional, highly selective, even finicky. If there was ever a time to put you and your wants and needs first, this is it.

You are absolutely *not* required to open your heart to everything just because the world feels like it's on fire.

In fact, **choosing wisely is one of the ways you stay well enough to keep showing up.**

You Still Own Your Body

Yes, your body has been politicized.
Yes, your identity may be debated.
Yes, your safety may be threatened.
Hell, your very right to exist may be up for debate.

And yet…
Your body still belongs to you.

You decide:

- When to rest

- What you eat

- Who you touch

- How you move

- What rituals nourish you

Even if the world disrespects your body, you do not have to.

Treat your body like sacred ground. Because it is.

Set the intention: My body, my voice, my actions and my breath are mine and I will use them in a way that best serves my soul.

This Is How We Reclaim Power

When you've been disempowered, the path back starts with *choosing what's yours*, again and again.

You don't have to fix everything.

But you do have the right—and the power—to decide how you show up in your own life.

Start there.
Start small.
Start with your breath, your words, your daily rhythm.

That's how we reclaim power: from the inside out.

***

Reflection Prompts:

1. What are three things I *can* control today, no matter what?

2. What helps me feel grounded in my body and spirit?

3. Where have I been giving away my power without meaning to?

4. What would it look like to reclaim one small boundary this week?

5. What do I want to *water* in my life—what deserves more of my attention?

PART III
STRENGTHENING THE HOPE MUSCLE

Chapter 7
Hope Is a Skill (And We're Going to Practice It)

Hope is the desire for something to happen.

I hope I get that promotion.
But you never apply because of fear of rejection.

I hope we have kind leaders.
But you have to show up and vote.

I hope someone reads this book.
I have to write it first!

We've been told that hope is something you either have, or you don't.

That it's a feeling that arises when things are good, and disappears when life gets hard.

But here's a mindset that will change your life:
Hope is not a feeling. Hope is a skill.
And like any skill, it can be taught, learned, practiced, and strengthened.

Especially when the world is heavy.
And the world is heavy now.
So, in the meantime, we gon' work on hope.

Why Hope Feels So Hard Right Now

Hope feels distant when:

- The news is bleak

- The systems are broken

- The leaders are cruel

- The future feels uncertain

- And your nervous system is running on fumes

But just because hope feels hard to reach doesn't mean it's gone.

You haven't lost hope. You may have just forgotten how to find it.

Do you remember back in Chapter 4, when I was talking about the news cycle? As I write this, our news cycle has been greatly sped up. There is *too much* news, and much of the news that exists has been manufactured. Many headlines are not really news, but distractions to keep us dizzied and unfocused. Dan Rather describes this as the "firehose effect"—a constant barrage of hateful and troubling headlines. "It's designed to overwhelm…" he says, "[so] we won't be able to keep up and so we stop trying."[1]

Don't meditate on headlines. Meditate on hope.

In this article, Mr. Rather also quotes writer Rebecca Solnit:

> "There is no alternative to persevering, and that does not require you to feel good. You can keep walking whether it's sunny or raining. Take care of yourself and remember that taking care of something else is an important

---

1   Rather, D. (2025, January 22). *The firehose effect.* The Firehose Effect: Don't Let (The) Deluge Stop You. https://steady.substack.com/p/the-firehose-effect

part of taking care of yourself, because you are interwoven with the ten trillion things in this single garment of destiny that has been stained and torn, but is still being woven and mended and washed."

He then adds his own message, which I really need you to hear:

"The dreams of our forefathers and mothers and our collective wills are being tested, strained, and torn. But they can withstand this test and be mended. Please keep in mind that four years of our 250-year history is just 1.6%. What's happening now will not break our great historical commitment to freedom and democracy. But the only way to the other side of where we are right now is through. We will get through together.

So be of hope and optimism."

Be of hope and optimism, take care of yourself, and take care of something else. Above all else, hold on to hope. It is how we get through dark times together.

What the Research Tells Us

The late Psychologist Charles Snyder was a leading researcher on hope. (It really is a science!) Dr. Snyder believed that hope is a cognitive state and he defined hope as "the belief that you can find pathways to your goals and become motivated to use those pathways."

According to Snyder's **Hope Theory**, real hope has three parts:

1. **A goal** – something you want

2. **A pathway** – a way (or many ways) to get there

3. **Agency** – the belief that you *can* take those steps

That's it. Hope is not just sitting around and wishing. It's believing that something better is possible and that you can play an active role in getting there.

The Truth About Hope

Hope is *not* wishful thinking.
It's not toxic positivity.
It is not pretending things are fine.
It is not ignoring pain or injustice.

Hope is the decision to believe that something better is still possible—*even if we don't see it yet.*

It's the choice to get up one more time.

To speak up, to rest, to plan, to build, to dream.

To believe in the possibility of tomorrow, even when today hurts.

I call the active work on the subject of hope **hoping skills**.

Hope as a Skill Means...

- You don't wait for hope to arrive, you *build* it.

- You don't have to feel hopeful to act with hope.

- You can create habits that make hope more accessible.

- Hope can become a *practice*, just like mindfulness, or prayer, or courage.

Hope isn't magic. It's maintenance.

How We Practice the Hoping Skill

You build hope by doing things that restore your connection to:

- Yourself
- Other humans and inhabitants of the planet
- The future
- The past
- A deeper purpose
- The truth

And you build your hope **on purpose**—not by accident, and not just when you feel like it.

Like any skill, the more you practice it, the stronger it gets. And even when the world tries to strip it from you, you can return to the practice again and again. You will develop unshakeable hope. Something they can never take away, no matter what they tell you.

Your Mini Hoping Skill Toolkit: A Simple Weekly Practice

Each week, ask yourself:

1. **What nourishes my hope?**

- Connection? Laughter? Silence? A good book? Helping someone else?

2. **What drains my hope?**

- Social media? Certain conversations? Unrealistic expectations?

3. **What can I do this week to refill my Hope Meter?**

- Small acts that remind you of your own power

4. **What can I imagine that I haven't given myself permission to want?**

- Let yourself dream again. Even if it scares you

5. **Who will I tell about my hopes to make them real?**

- Keep your hope alive. Give it air like a fire needs to take hold. Speak it. Write it. Live it.

I know this is hard, but this is healing. There will be days when you look at this and scoff. You might even find yourself reading these words one day and thinking *what a joke*.

And that's real.

That's *100*.

But I did not pretend to come here to tell you this was easy.

I am telling you it is essential.

And with all things that are not easy, but essential, you have to put in the work.

You have to work to keep your hope meter on high. Be prepared to answer the scoff head on with something like, "*This is not a joke. This is my one precious life.*"

Hope doesn't erase struggle.
But it does give you strength in the meantime.

Hope empowers you to meet struggle with dignity, resilience, and vision.
You were made to hope.
You just need to remember how.

***

Reflection Prompts:

1. What does "hope" mean to me right now?

2. When do I feel most connected to hope?

3. What gets in the way of hope in my daily life?

4. What are some small ways I can practice the Hoping Skill this week?

5. If I believed things *could* get better, what would I do next?

Chapter 8
Dreams Are Not a Luxury. They Are a Lifeline

Okay, so, this is my thing… So give me this one chapter, okay? I am the dream lady. I'm a professional dreamer and quite proud of it. My parents were hippies. Real hippies who wore flowers in their hair and got married at the courthouse while all their friends were sprawled out all over the courthouse lawn.

And one parent was Black and one parent was white. They married in 1970. I grew up in Kentucky, a state that didn't even repeal its own anti-miscegenation statute until 1974. So, I got all this dreaming and hope stuff honestly.

But somewhere along the way, many of us—most of us—got the message that dreaming was frivolous.

Selfish. Unrealistic. A complete waste of time. Even childish.

We got the message that we should "be practical," and that dreaming is anything but that. That *now* isn't the time. (*It's never the time.*) That dreaming is only for the privileged, the lucky, the rich. (*It is not.*)

Here's the message the system does not want you to get:

Dreaming is not a luxury.
Dreaming is a survival skill.
Dreaming is hope in action.
Dreaming is how we reach for something better,
even when the world tells us to settle for less.

And we need it now more than ever.

The System Benefits When We Stop Dreaming

If you're exhausted, overwhelmed, and scared, of course you're not dreaming.

That's the point.

The more oppressed, overworked, and disillusioned we become, the less likely we are to imagine new possibilities. And without imagination, there is no will to change.

But here's the secret:
Every movement that changed the world began with someone who dared to dream anyway.

- Someone dreamed of a school that welcomed every child.

- Someone dreamed of a country where their vote counted.

- Someone dreamed that women could own bank accounts, credit cards, and property.

- Someone dreamed of justice, equality, and rest.

If they could dream under those conditions, *so can we.*

Your Dreams Are Sacred Data

Your dreams tell you what matters. What is opportune. What you're meant for.
Dreams are *revelation*.

Dreams point us to a version of ourselves we haven't lived yet, but were always meant to.

You don't have to dream something huge.
You just have to let yourself *want* again.

You're Not Broken if You've Stopped Dreaming

If you can't remember the last time you felt excited about the future…
If your imagination feels flatlined…
If you've been stuck in survival mode so long you've forgotten what it feels like to want…

Please hear this: **You are not broken**.

You've been surviving. You've been adapting. You've been enduring things in life that no one should have to.

But your dreams are still *in* you. They are still there.

Even when you can't hear them speaking to you.

Buried maybe. Bruised, even. But not gone.
They are waiting. And they're patient.

You can begin again. Today.

Dreaming in the Meantime

You don't have to wait for the world to be fixed before
you give yourself permission to dream.

In fact, the dream is *part of the fix.* I need your help
spreading the word about that!

Let your dreaming be:

- Messy
- Unfinished
- Soft
- Hopeful
- Scary
- Yours

Dream without guilt.
Dream with others.
Dream in a community.
Dream when you're tired.

Dream because the world needs what only you have the ability to imagine.

***

Reflection Prompts:

1. What dreams did I give up because I believed I wasn't ready, worthy, or allowed?

2. What do I miss that I haven't admitted out loud?

3. If nothing was holding me back, what would I want next?

4. What feels like a small dream I can move toward now?

5. How does dreaming make me feel in my body? Free? Afraid? Alive?

Chapter 9
You Were Made for This Moment

Right now—without any hesitation—put one hand on your chest and the other hand on your belly. Take a deep breath all the way in for four seconds. Hold it for four seconds. Then exhale all the way out for four seconds. While you do this say, to yourself or out loud, "I was made for this moment."

You can do this anytime from anywhere.

If negative voices pop up in your mind while doing this, say, "I do not have time for negative voices. I am in a positive space. I am returning to my positive space. I am going to stay in my positive space. I was made for this moment. I was made for this moment."

There's a voice inside you that will say: *This is too much. I'm not equipped for this. I can't possibly handle this mess.*

But there's another voice, quieter but deeper.
It says: You are here now for a reason.

And that voice is telling the truth. The other voice is not.

Did you ever watch old cartoons like Bugs Bunny, where he would have an angel on one shoulder and a devil on the other and they would both be talking to him? They both had their own worldview and were full of advice about what he should do next. The angel is the truth teller. The devil is the lie. Listen to the angel. Listen to the voice that makes you feel good.

The more you silence the voice that makes you feel bad, the quieter that voice gets.
It takes practice, but you can do this. **It works.**

Entire systems have invested in you *not* believing this. That's because they need you to show up for them, so they cannot have you believing that you can also show up for yourself.

You don't have to be fearless.

You don't have to be perfect.
You just have to show up. As you are. Right now.

Because you were made for this moment.

How Do I Know?

Because you're still here. And that's the truth.

Despite the grief.
Despite the burnout.
Despite the chaos and cruelty and headlines and harm and all the hate. *You* are still here.

You keep waking up. You keep caring.
You keep showing up in ways that may look small but are anything *but*.

And the world needs that.
The world needs *you*.

Crisis Creates the Call

Throughout history, ordinary people—tired people, scared people, imperfect people—have stood in moments just like this and made impossible things happen.

They didn't feel ready, either.

But the moment was real, and so they rose.

That's exactly what's happening now.

The moment is calling.
Not just for protest or survival, but for healing. And for dreaming. For courage. For clarity. For *truth*.

This Isn't the End.
This is the middle

It may feel like everything is falling apart.
But what if it's all falling into place?

This moment is breaking the illusion.
What needs to collapse is collapsing.

"Things must be revealed." Remember that?
What if you were born *not to avoid the storm*—but to plant seeds in its aftermath?

You don't have to know how it ends.
You just have to choose to still care—to still hope—in the meantime.

You Are More Powerful Than You Remember

Remember when you were eight years old and believed you could fly? This is who you are at your core, before the messages of the world got to you. Before those messages set in. You were a rock star. That rock star did not go anywhere. It may be harder to hear the music now, but the music is still playing.

Tune out the lie.
Turn up the truth.

This is an intention.
You are powerful, not because you have all the answers.
But because you *ask the right questions.*
Because you still dream. You still try. You still love.

This moment isn't too big for you.
You were born with gifts and truth that this moment desperately needs.

Even when you don't feel brave, your hope is.

Even when you feel unseen, your presence matters.

Even when you want to disappear, you being here changes the world. Just ask a friend—a good friend—and you will see exactly what you mean to this world.

You Don't Have to Save the World Alone

This moment is too big for any one of us. But it's not too big for *all of us*.

You don't need to be the hero.
You just need to take your place—whatever and wherever that is.

The artist.
The healer.
The parent.
The teacher.
The neighbor.
The truth-teller.

Your role matters.
Your story matters.
Your light matters.

Don't bury it. Bring it.

You were made for this moment.

***

Reflection Prompts:

1. What makes me believe I was born with purpose?

2. What unique gifts do I bring to this world—even if they're quiet?

3. What do I want this chapter of my life to stand for?

4. What can I do to trust myself more in hard moments?

5. If I fully believed I was made for this moment, what would I do differently?

PART IV
MOVING FORWARD WITHOUT GIVING UP

Chapter 10
How to Keep Going When It Feels Like Nothing Changes

This might be the hardest part of all:

When you've protested, written, called, marched, cried, rested, hoped; and still, the world doesn't seem to budge.

The executive orders are issued.
The bills still pass.

The cruelty still happens.

The people in power still pretend not to hear.

And you wonder: What's the point?

If that's where you are, take a breath.

You're not alone.

You're not failing.

And you're not wrong to feel tired.

But don't give up.

Because what's happening *matters*, even when you can't see it yet.

Remember: there has always been a battle between good and evil.

Always has been.

Always will be.

But resistance works.

And the truth is the light.

Hold on to these words from Dr. Martin Luther King, Jr.:

"The arc of the moral universe is long, but it bends toward justice."

The bend just may well be me and you pushing it. It certainly was helped along by Dr. King.

The Change You Can't See

So much of what truly transforms us happens below the surface.

Seeds grow in the dark, they keep pushing through before they ever see a drop of sun. Bones heal in silence.

Movements swell underground—before they ever reach the street.

The same is true of this moment.
Your actions, your healing, your hope—they *are* working.

Just because you don't see the ripple yet doesn't mean it isn't there.

You are planting something.
Keep going.

The Myth of Quick Wins

Social media trained us to expect instant results. (Wigs to replace the look of your natural hair, lashes that touch the sky, weight that falls off in days, even a dance routine you are supposed to be able to learn in minutes.)

But justice? Healing? Systems change?
They move like glaciers. Like roots. Like tides.

But they move.

The people who brought us through the Civil Rights movement, the voting rights era, the LGBTQIA+ movement, the fight for disability justice didn't see all the fruit of their labor.

But they showed up anyway. Because they knew:

Sometimes you fight not for the outcome, but for *the integrity of your soul*.

You fight because it's *right*.
You love because it's *true*.
You hope because it's *yours to protect*.

That's why you do it. That's why you get up every day and start again. It's not because you see change. It's because you don't.

Keep pushing. You are a seed in soil.

You are part of the bend toward justice.

Sustainable Hope = Pacing + Purpose

Burnout happens when you think you *have* to do everything.
Sustainable hope happens when you remember:

- You are one person, not the entire movement.

- Rest *is* a part of resistance.

- Boundaries *are* strategy.

- Joy is non-negotiable.

- Faith—in yourself, in the future—is renewable.

You keep going not because the change is easy,
but because *you're becoming the kind of person who keeps going.*

Even the Smallest Spark Still Lights a Path

Don't underestimate the power of showing up:

- For your community

- For your children

- For your body

- For your art

- For your truth

Your consistency is a form of protest.

You did not fall for the propaganda.

The firehose did not take you down.

Your joy is a kind of revolution.

And your endurance is a *signal to the future* that says:

"We were here. And we never stopped believing something better was possible."

Or in other words: "Illegitimi non carborundum."

***

Reflection Prompts:

1. Where in my life have I seen change, even if it was slow?

2. What sustains me when I feel like giving up?

3. How do I measure progress in ways that aren't just external?

4. What does it look like to pace myself for the long road?

5. What do I want future generations to say I helped make possible?

Chapter 11
Building Communities of Care

There is only so far you can go alone.

Yes, hope is a skill.
Yes, dreams matter.
Yes, you are powerful.

But if you've ever felt like you were screaming into the wind or carrying the weight of the world on your own shoulders, there is a reason.

We were never meant to heal in isolation.

We are wired for connection.
And when systems fail us, *community is what saves us.*

Why We Need Each Other

In moments of injustice, fear, and despair, the world will tell you to fend for yourself.

But the truth is:

Another very revolutionary thing you can do is build something safe.
Something soft. Something rooted in love.
Especially when everything outside of you feels hard.

We build communities of care, not as a luxury,but as a necessity.

Care is not the opposite of activism.
Care *is* activism.

What Is a Community of Care?

A community of care is:

- The friend who checks in without needing a reason

- The group chat where you can show up exactly as you are
- The Zoom call that turns into therapy, laughter, and prayer
- The meal train for a grieving neighbor
- A school teacher who lets kids eat in their classroom when the cafeteria is overwhelming
- Picking up a grocery order for an elder or the sick
- A group of parents who rotate babysitting nights
- The protest group that knows when it's time to rest
- The healing circle, the safe house, the Sunday dinner
- A book festival or club

It's not about how many people you have. It's about the space you create.

How to Start Building a Community of Care (Even Now)

You don't need healed people.
You just need **willing people.**

People willing to:

- Hold space
- Apologize and repair
- Make time
- Protect each other's softness
- Share their light
- Follow through

Start with what you need.
Start by offering what you can.
Start small. Start real.

I had a dream of starting the Louisville Book Festival. And I made that dream come true. This has now turned out to be a pretty large event. The amount of people who have become friends, vacationed together, continued to write more books together, and returned to the festival every year is inspiring. Your action does not have to be that. You don't have to host a massive book festival. A Little Library has a huge impact. You don't have to build an entire Little Library. Maybe you make it your personal mission to keep the one closest to you stocked.

Start small. Start real. There are so many ways to build community or to support some that already exist.

What a Community of Care Offers:

- Safety when the world feels unsafe

- Witness when you feel invisible

- Accountability without shame

- Celebration when hope feels far away

- Company when the world seeks to isolate you

- Support that feels genuine

- Gentle reminders that *you're not crazy. You're alive and awake in a world that gaslights your humanity.*

When we care for each other, we become harder to control.
Harder to silence.
Harder to break.

We *know* we are not alone. We become a force.

If you ever need a refresher course on hope, sit down to have a chat with the very old or the very young. Hope lives within their spirits boldly.

Protect the circle.

Once you build community, protect it. Nurture it. Let it evolve.

Don't wait until crisis hits. Make care a practice, not a panic.

And remember:

You don't need to do it all. You just need to *not* do it alone.

***

Reflection Prompts:

1. Who in my life makes me feel safe, seen, or stronger?

2. What does it mean to "build a circle of care" in this season of my life?

3. Where could I offer care—without burning out?

4. What kind of support do I need that I've been afraid to ask for?

5. How can I help others feel less alone, starting this week?

Chapter 12
Protecting Your Light... in the Meantime

You've made it this far.

Through the heartbreak.

Through the headlines.

Through the grief, the anger, the numbness.

Through the quiet, daily choice to keep going.

Now, as we near the end of this book—but not the end of this journey—there is one final truth to remember:

Your light is sacred. It is a gift given to you, for moments like this.

And it is your responsibility to protect it.

This World Wasn't Built for Your Radiance. *Light It Up Anyway.*

We live in a world that profits from your exhaustion.

It benefits from your self-doubt.
It thrives when your joy is gone.

Somehow, they think there is more joy for them when there is less joy for you.

Promise me friend... This is me talking to you... *Promise me* you will not let them take this from you.

Write the words **joy and hope** on a piece of paper. Fold it up and put it in your pocket. Take it with you everywhere you go as a reminder that these are yours and they are with you always.

You will grow stronger. I promise you. But the opposite is also true.
The despair grows stronger every time you buy into the lie that you don't matter.

But you do.
I know it and they know it.

You matter.
Your peace matters.
Your joy matters.

Your healing matters.
Your *light* matters.

You are not too much.
You are not too soft.
You are not too hopeful.
You are not too anything.

You are exactly what this moment needs.

The Light Doesn't Stay On by Accident

You can't just *hope* your light stays on.

You have to *tend* to it.

This means:

- Saying no when your gut says no
- Resting without guilt
- Nourishing what brings you back to life
- Choosing people who don't dim you
- Turning down the volume of chaos in your life
- Letting silence be a teacher, not a threat
- Finding and celebrating joy

This world may not always protect you.
But you can still protect *yourself.*

That is not selfish. That's real.

As a therapist, I have so many women who come and lay on my couch and tell me what pieces of crap they feel like because they "did nothing" yesterday. Or last weekend. Or last week. Or this month. Or this year.

Let's change the language we use when we talk about this.

It is not that we "did nothing" yesterday. You know what we did yesterday? We recharged yesterday, that's what we did.

In nature, everything has a season. Everything. And we are a part of nature too. A tree works hard in the spring to produce new and longer limbs. It grows leaves and maybe fruits or nuts or seeds. In summer, it shines in all its glory, the most full it will be all year long. Then in the autumn it starts winding down. There is nothing you can do to stop the leaves from drying out and withering. Eventually the leaves fall off. All evidence of any production is gone. For three to four months a year the tree lies dormant, and no one ever asks why. We accept this as a part of life.

So why don't we accept this in ourselves? We are as much a part of nature as that tree. Ashes to ashes.

Dust to dust. We cannot produce 365 days a year any more than that tree can.

Everything has a season.

When you find yourself in need of a recharge, take it. You won't be able to produce what you really need to, until you do. Take the recharge and come back better. Just like that tree.

Build Your Light-Protection Plan

You wouldn't leave your house without a coat in the winter.

So don't leave your spirit unguarded in a storm.

Your light needs:

- Boundaries
- Rest
- Creative expression
- Soulful people
- Soft places
- Laughter

- Tears
- A little bit of an attitude
- Truth over noise
- Hope over hustle

You need a personal plan. A plan that you create. This is how you keep your hope meter filled.

What brings you back to you?

A Ritual for the Meantime

At the end of each hard day, ask:

- *What did I protect today?*
- *What protected me?*
- *What can I let go of now?*

If you want to take this exercise a step further, find a quiet space, light a candle and answer these questions in a journal. This will help you make this a practice and you will be amazed when you look back at your journey through the power of journaling.

Make your favorite warm drink. Spend time in your own mind, searching your own heart.

You don't need to have it all figured out.

You just need a light that's still burning.

Even an ember is enough.

The Meantime Doesn't Have the Final Word

The meantime is the middle.
The meantime is not your destiny or your final destination.
Can you think of any better time to build *you*?
This is how we are going to make it through the middle.
We are going to get to our destiny and our dreams.
We will not give up on them.
We are very actively living in the cognitive state of hope.

Say that last line out loud.

You were not made to live in survival mode.
This moment—the meantime—is real.
It's hard. It's heavy.
But it's not the whole story.

You are still becoming.
You are still building.
You are still believing.

And in all of it, your light is still glowing.

You've done divine work just by arriving here.
On this page.
In this space.

Protect your light.
Pass it on.
And never stop believing that it's not over.

It is not over.

Are you breathing?

Then it is not over.

***

Reflection Prompts:

1. What parts of me shine the brightest when I feel safe and seen?

2. How can I tell when my light is dimming?

3. What practices restore my inner light?

4. Who or what helps me remember who I am?

5. What's one small ritual I can create to honor and protect my peace?

PART V
IN THE
MEANTIME—
LIVING THE
LEGACY OF HOPE

Chapter 13
The Spiral of Setbacks and What to Do When You Lose Hope Again

We all have bad days. It's gonna happen. Accept that and get ready for bad days so they don't catch you off guard.

Break the habit and the automatic go to of saying, "I quit," or "I give up."

Instead say, "I'll see you tomorrow, tomorrow."

Sometimes hope fades.

Even after the healing.
Even after the wins.
Even after the rituals and affirmations and actions.

There will still be days—maybe even weeks—when everything you've learned, everything you've practiced, suddenly feels far away. Like none of it ever happened.

This is not failure.
This is *human*.

Hope (Like Healing) Isn't a Straight Line

You can know better and still forget.
You can feel strong one day and fragile the next.
You can believe in yourself in the morning and feel like a fraud by night.

This doesn't mean you're broken.
It means you're alive.
You are breathing.

Healing and growth are not linear. They're *spirals*. Sometimes the spiral goes up. Sometimes the spiral goes down. You will revisit old fears. You'll face familiar pain. You'll even be triggered. Sometimes it feels like you're going in circles. But you're not. With each round of the spiral, you're coming back with new tools. New awareness. A little more wisdom than the last time.

That's progress. Progress you only get because of the spiral. Learn from the fear, the pain, the triggers. These are lessons, not last stops. Don't give up because of them. Persist anyway.

Why We Slide Back

Setbacks happen when:

- You're emotionally drained
- You face trauma or triggers
- You forget to rest
- You haven't had enough water
- You isolate yourself
- You expect too much of yourself, too soon
- You become enraged by ignorance or inhumanity

- The world throws a fresh wave of injustice at you

- You have not allowed any joy into your day

These moments are not invitations to give up. These moments are invitations to check on you. A call to *return*.

Return to your breath.
Return to your rituals.
Return to what you know: **this will not stand. You will rise again.**

What to Do When You Feel Yourself Spiraling

1. Name It

Say it out loud or write it down: *"I feel myself spiraling."* This interrupts the autopilot of shame and re-centers you in awareness.

2. Pause and Breathe

One slow breath. Then another. You don't have to fix everything. Just *be* with yourself. Feel your feet flat on the floor. Center yourself.

3. Show Yourself Mercy

Self-compassion is your lifeline here. Remind yourself: "I've been here before. I already beat this feeling before. I'm 'bout to beat it again."

Breathe.

All the way in. Hold it for four seconds. All the way out. And again. "Yep. I'm about to beat this again. I am a rock star."

4. Challenge the Thought Loop

What story am I telling myself right now?
Is it true, or just the story I'm used to?
If it's not a true story, let's write a new one. A story that is helpful to my healing and true.

5. Return to Your Light

Go back to one small thing that worked to lift you before:

- A song
- A journal
- A prayer
- A promise
- A text to someone safe
- A moment of stillness

- A letter someone sent to you

- A saved voicemail that makes you feel heard and seen

- A page in this book

This is your practice. And practice means you keep showing up. Day in, day out, you show up to check on you.

You Don't Lose Everything Just Because You Forgot For a Minute

You are still growing—even if you're growing through grief, resistance, or silence.
You are still worthy—even if the light flickers.
You are still capable of hope—even if that hope is quiet today.

***

Reflection Prompts:

1. What does it feel like in my body when I'm spiraling?

2. What signs tell me I need to slow down?

3. What has helped me return to hope in the past?

4. What do I most need to hear in the middle of a setback?

5. What do I want to remember next time this happens?

Chapter 14
Hope at the Ballot Box and Reclaiming Power in Civic Life

There is great power in voting. If there was no power in voting, people would not have full-time jobs solely dedicated to figuring out how to take it from you.

Voting is one of the greatest and most powerful rights you have.

In the United States of America, in 2025, we have the right to vote.

Voting doesn't always feel powerful.
It doesn't always feel like enough.
And after everything we've lived through—leaders we didn't choose, policies that harm the most vulnerable,

a system that often seems so heavily weighted—it's easy to wonder:

What's the point?

The fact is, voting is not the whole story.
But it *is* one of the few times folks who hold office have to listen.

There are people who are afraid of your vote. It *does* make them listen. Even when they win, they hear your vote.

Your vote talks. Don't ever forget that. And your vote is powerful. *Very* powerful.

When It Feels Like Your Vote Doesn't Matter

If you've voted and watched your candidates lose…
If you've shown up and still seen injustice win…
If you've watched communities stripped of rights in spite of record turnout…

You're not wrong to feel discouraged.

But you're still not powerless.

There is no perfect system.
But there is a reason there are groups of people trying

to make it harder for you to vote.

A reason they spread confusion.

A reason they gerrymander. Suppress. Distract. Block.

Because your voice—especially *your voting voice*—has power.

And they know it.

You need to know it too.

Voting Is Hope in Action

Voting is more than picking a president.

It's:

- Electing school board members who decide what your kids learn
- Choosing judges who rule on police reform and reproductive rights
- Picking city council members who decide where your tax money goes
- Choosing mayors and governors who set the tone for your entire state

We talk a lot about systems.
But voting is one of the few *system-level levers* we can pull regularly.

It's not enough on its own.
But it is *never nothing.*

Vote Because You're Angry. Vote Because You Care. Vote Because You *Can*. Vote because it is your *right*.

It is deflating to hear people say they don't vote because the outcome of the vote does not affect them. This is a lie that was floated to you from some platform and you fell for it.

You fell for the propaganda.

Nothing could be further from the truth. I personally think it also helps to **deeply remember** that people really did die for your right to vote today. People who never in their lives got to know what it felt like to cast a vote, *fought and died*, so you could. It was that serious.

You don't have to feel hopeful or patriotic to vote.
You don't even have to believe in the system.
You just have to believe that your voice deserves to be counted.

Voting is not a performance of belief in a perfect government.

It's a declaration of refusal.

Refusal to disappear, or to stay silent. A refusal to let others decide your future *without* you. You have a say. Your vote matters.

In the 2024 Presidential election, more people did not vote than the number of people who elected the President that year. But you believe your vote does not matter. An estimated 89 million Americans, about 36% of the country's voting-eligible population, did not vote in the 2024 Presidential election.[2]

Do you want to build a community? Build a voting community. Teach citizenship and the power of voting as a class.

Tell them the story of Rubén Salazar. Rubén was one of the most well-known Latino journalists of the twentieth century. He was also a civil rights advocate who wrote about police brutality, political disenfranchisement, and the power of civic participation—especially voting—as a path toward justice. Salazar was killed in 1970 by a police officer

---

2   *2024 was a landslide...for "did not vote."* Environmental Voter Project. (2024, November 5). https://www.environmentalvoter.org/updates/2024-was-landslidefor-did-not-vote

while covering a peaceful anti-war protest in East Los Angeles. His death became a symbol of the silencing of truth-tellers—and a reminder of how dangerous it can be to speak up for your community... *and how essential it still is.*

But I tell his story here to remember Rubén's hope, and the hope he had in voting. When asked during an interview if he thought that the Vietnam War would throw the country into a revolution, he replied, "I think the United States is traditionally a revolutionary country... We are going to overthrow some of our institutions, but in the way that Americans have always done it: through the ballot, through public consensus. That's a revolution. That is a real revolution."

Rubén's life lives on. He is a real example of courage in the face of oppression (also known as hope), and a painful reminder that while these systems were not built for all of us, they now belong to all of us.

We can't give up. We can't check out.

Rubén's legacy tells us:

- **Voting is power**—and power is always challenged
- Journalism and truth-telling matter—especially in hard times

- **Hope isn't soft—it's resistance**

Voting is our revolution. Teach *that*.

What Else You Can Do Besides Voting

If you feel like "just voting" isn't enough—good. It's not.

That's why we:

- Help others register
- Show up for local meetings
- Support candidates who align with our values
- Write postcards
- Make calls
- Donate what we can, be it money, time, eyes and ears.
- Teach our children the power of civic voice

This is long-haul hope.
Something we have not invested anywhere near enough in.
This is how we shape the next generation.
This is how we take the long way home.

***

Reflection Prompts:

1. When have I felt most powerful as a citizen?

2. What discourages me about voting? What might reframe it?

3. What local issue do I care about deeply?

4. How can I use my voice between elections?

5. What civic legacy do I want to pass down?

Chapter 15
What If I Need More Help? When the Book Isn't Enough

Sometimes, the storm gets louder than the tools we've been given.

Sometimes, no matter how many pages you underline, how many breaths you take, how many rituals you return to, it still feels like too much.

If you're reading this chapter with tears in your eyes, a lump in your throat, or numbness you can't quite shake…

Let me say this first:

You are not weak.
You are not failing.
And you are not alone.

There Comes a Point When Books Aren't Enough

Books can hold us.
They can inspire us.
They can give language to the pain we've never been able to name.

But sometimes, even the most powerful book is not a substitute for the *power of being heard*—in real time, by a human being who is trained to help you carry what's too heavy for one heart alone.

That's when therapy, support groups, or healing communities become essential.

How to Know If You Need More Support

You deserve and need more support if you:

- Feel overwhelmed most days and can't explain why

- Are experiencing panic, chronic sadness, or numbness

- Can't sleep, eat, or function in your usual way

- Are isolating from people who care about you

- Feel like nothing brings you joy

- Are struggling with harmful thoughts or behaviors

- Have survived trauma you've never processed

- Just want someone to help you make sense of what you're going through

Needing more help doesn't mean this book didn't work.

It means *you're ready for your next level of care*.

You can have many tools in your toolbox. This book is one. Therapy is another.

What Therapy Really Is (and Isn't)

Therapy isn't just for people in crisis.

And it's not just for "crazy" people, whatever that means.

The truth is, we're all a little crazy.

Therapy is for anyone ready to learn more about themselves, break patterns, breathe fully, heal deeper, and live with more freedom in their heart and in their mind.

It's not:

- A sign of weakness

- A last resort

- Something to be ashamed of

It *is*:

- A safe space to unpack what hurts

- A partnership for healing

- A brave act of self-respect

And for many, especially in marginalized communities, it is an act of *defiance* to say:

"I will not carry this alone. I deserve to be whole."

Therapy is hope in action.

Finding the Right Kind of Help

Every person is different. The key is finding what works *for you.*

Here are some options:

- **Individual therapy** (in-person or online)

- **Group therapy** (grief groups, trauma-informed spaces, etc.)

- **Faith-based counseling** (when aligned with your beliefs)

- **Crisis support** (hotlines, peer warm lines, chat/text options)

- **Healing circles and affinity spaces** for Black, LGBTQIA+, disabled, immigrant, or other identity-based communities

You deserve a helper who understands not just your pain, but *your context.* Your culture. Your story. Make the call. Interview your therapist. Don't feel like you need to stick with the first one you meet.

You Are Not Too Far Gone

There is no "too late."
There is no "too broken."
There is only you—and the next brave step forward.

That's all you have to focus on right now.
The next step.

You've already done something courageous by reading this book.
If you feel like you've hit the limit of what you can do alone, that's not weakness.
That's wisdom.

***

Reflection Prompts:

1. What parts of me still feel unseen, even after all this work?

2. What scares me about asking for help? What might happen if I did?

3. Who could walk with me into the next level of healing?

4. How do I define safety, and what kind of support would feel safe to me?

5. What's one small step I could take toward deeper care this week?

Chapter 16
Raising Hopeful Kids in a Heavy World

Why This Chapter Matters— Even If You Don't Have Kids

I know not everyone reading this book is a parent.

But every single one of us is part of the world our children are inheriting. The children of the world belong to all of us. Whether we birth them, teach them, mentor them, love them, or simply share a sidewalk with them, **we are shaping their future.** And in turn, they will shape *ours.*

This chapter is for everyone who wants to believe that the future can still be good, and that we all have a role in building it.

Children are watching us. They're watching what we normalize. What we accept. What we resist. What we hope for.

But even more than that, they *are* our future.

- These kids will be the voters when we are old and there are not as many of us.

- They will be the ones running for office, writing laws, leading companies, shaping policy, and deciding what kind of world we get to grow old in.

- They will be the ones building or dismantling the systems we're fighting for or against right now.

- And yes, they will be the ones funding Social Security and deciding how to care for *us.*

The way we treat children today—the way we speak to them, invest in them, and nurture their hope—will come back to us in every possible form.

If we teach them to tune out, to give up, to believe that nothing ever gets better,we are not just harming *them*. We're harming *tomorrow*.

But if we model truth, accountability, care, and courage...
If we show them that hope is a skill, and healing is a path, and power can be used to protect...
Then we plant seeds we may not live to see bloom, but that will grow long after we're gone.

We don't just raise children.
We raise future leaders. Future caregivers. Future voters. Future protectors of democracy.
We raise the world we'll grow old in.

That's why this chapter is here.
Because their future is still being written.
And so is ours.

They're watching.
Even when we don't think they understand.
Even when we try to shield them.
Even when we're breaking inside ourselves—

The children are watching.

And what they need most from us is not perfection.
Not certainty.
Not forced cheer.

They need *truth* spoken with love.
They need *safety* without silence.
They need to know that even in a world full of heartbreak—hope still belongs to them.

Kids Can Feel the Weight, Too

Children sense the tension in the air. They overhear our worries.
They absorb our emotions before they even have words for their own.

They ask hard questions:

- *Why do people get shot at school?*
- *Why is that person homeless?*
- *Why is that man on the news yelling?*
- *Why are you crying?*

And we panic, wondering how to answer. How much is too much? How do we protect their innocence without lying?

Tell them the truth. But don't forget the hope.

What Hope Looks Like for a Child

Hope isn't just a big idea. *It's something they practice.*

When a child:

- Tries again after falling
- Believes they can make a friend
- Imagines a different future
- Asks why something is unfair
- Speaks up for a friend being mistreated
- Shows kindness when it's hard
- Has a dream and shares it

That's hope.

And you can nurture it.

How to Talk to Children About Hard Things Without Crushing Them

1. **Start with safety.**

   Let them know: "I'm here. You're safe to feel what you feel."

2. **Be honest in age-appropriate ways.**

   You don't need all the answers. You just need to be real.

3. **Ask what they already know.**

   Kids are often trying to make sense of fragmented info. Start there.

4. **Validate their emotions.**

   Say: "That *is* scary," or "It's okay to feel sad." This builds emotional literacy.

5. **Always bring it back to what we can do.**

   Empowerment is the antidote to despair.

Teaching the Hoping Skill to Kids

You've already taught them to brush their teeth and tie their shoes.

You can help them learn how to hope, too.

Teach them to ask:

- *What do I need today?*
- *What helps me feel better?*
- *What's something kind I can do?*
- *What is one small thing I believe in?*
- *What am I looking forward to the most?*

Practice as a family:

- Share one hopeful thing from the day at dinner

- Create a "Hope Jar" with notes of joy, dreams, or gratitude. Read some of these once a week as a group or when you all need a little fuel for your light

- Watch uplifting shows or read books with stories of courage and change

- Let them dream without correcting or downsizing their vision

Hope grows in homes where hope is spoken out loud.

You Don't Have to Have it All "Right." You Just Have to be Present

Some days you'll lose your temper.
Some days you'll feel like you have nothing left to give.
Some days the world will break your heart.

But when they see you show up for them again,
If you keep holding space for their questions and their dreams,
If you tell them, *"Even when the world is hard, you're not alone…"*

If you practice saying together, *"I'll see you tomorrow, tomorrow,"*

Then you're raising a hopeful child.

And that's world-changing work.

***

Reflection Prompts:

1. What do I want the children in my life to believe about the world?

2. What's one thing I learned as a child that I want to *unlearn* for them?

3. How do I model hope in front of the children watching me?

4. What's one small ritual I can start to build hope at home?

5. What do I want my children/students to say about how I showed up during this time?

Chapter 17
You Are the Continuation

If you've made it to this point, I want you to take a breath.

A deep one.

Let it fill your chest.
Let it remind you that you're still here.
Still breathing. Still hoping. Still trying.

That alone makes you part of something truly sacred.

This life is special. Your breath is meaningful.

You Were Never Meant to Just Survive This Life

This world will try to convince you that survival is the goal.
That if you make it through the day, that's enough.
And some days, it is.

But I want you to know:

You were never meant to just survive.
You were meant to *continue*.
To carry forward the wisdom, light, softness, vision, courage, and love that existed before you, and will exist after you.

You are the vessel.

You are the change.

You Are Part of a Lineage of Hope

Every dreamer, healer, truth-teller, and justice seeker who came before you has passed the baton.

Maybe you didn't ask for it.
Maybe you didn't feel ready.

Maybe the world feels too broken for you to do anything with it.

But here you are, holding the light anyway.

You are the continuation of:

- The ancestors who survived so you could be born
- The protestors who stood so you could vote
- The teachers who taught so you could question
- The mothers, aunties, and neighbors who whispered, *"Keep going, baby. Keep going."*

Their stories did not end.
They live in you.

And one day, someone will say *your* name as the one who helped them keep going, too.

That's how powerful you are.

My mother started a theater company in Louisville, Kentucky in the 1980s. I recently shared a memory of her and several people commented on how influential she was to their careers as young actors. My mother passed away twenty-two years ago, and yet, people are invoking her name and the light she helped grow in them, *decades* later.

Your life is a light. Share it with someone else.

You Get to Shape What Comes Next

This book doesn't close with a solution.
That's because the solution is you.

You are the continuation of every quiet revolution.
Every candle lit in the dark.
Every book passed from one generation to the next.
Every hard conversation that made someone feel seen.
Every dream you dared to keep alive.
Every ripple that rebounds because you dared make a splash.
No matter how tired, no matter how scared—

You are not the end of the story.
You are the turning point.

Keep the Fire Lit

There will still be hard days.
There will still be spirals.
There will still be mornings when the fog returns.

But now you have a path back to yourself.

And you are not alone.

***

Closing Reflection Prompts:

1. What has this book stirred or shifted in me?

2. What chapter do I want to carry into my everyday life?

3. What legacy do I want to leave behind—with my words, my care, my presence?

4. Who do I want to become from here?

5. What does it mean to be *the continuation*?

Appendices

A Blessing for the Meantime

May you never forget the strength it took to get here—
not just the big things, but all the quiet ways you kept going.

May you stop beating yourself up for being tired.
You've been carrying a lot, for a long time.

May you always remember that there's something good inside you—
even if the world has tried to wear it down.

May this not be the end of your hope,
but the beginning of the world it was always meant to help build.

May you find strength again in the middle
and steady hope in the meantime.

Book Club Questions

Spark meaningful conversation, reflection, and *community* for healing, grounding, and holding on to hope

Opening Questions

1. **What made you want to read this book right now?**

   What were you hoping to find in it?

2. **What chapter or moment felt like it was written just for you?**

   Why did it hit so deeply?

3. **How would you describe "the meantime" in your own life?**

   What does it feel like to live in this space between despair and hope?

Breathe Section Questions

4. **Which grounding tool or breathing practice did you try—and what happened when you did?**

   Did anything surprise you?

5. **When stress takes over, what does your body usually do?**

   How has that awareness shifted for you?

Closing Question

6. **Who in your life needs this book—and how will you share it with them?**

Find the complete list of book club questions in the free download here:

Journal Prompts

Companion to the book club questions or individual reflection

Breathe – Ground Yourself in the Present

1. **When was the last time I felt calm in my body?**

   What was different about that moment, and what helped create it?

2. **Which breathing or grounding exercise helped me the most—and how did I feel after trying it?**

3. **What does it feel like to pause and remind myself: "I am safe right now"?**

   What changes in me when I say those words out loud?

Feel – Acknowledge What's Real

4. **What emotion have I been trying to avoid—and why?**

5. **What's one thing I've needed to hear from someone lately, but haven't?**

   What would it feel like to say those words to myself?

(Access the complete 21-day journal prompt guide in the free download on our website.)

One Promise

Write at least one promise to yourself here:

_____

_____

_____

_____

_____

_____

_____

_____

_____

_____

_____

_____

In the Meantime Tools

Quick Exercises to Ground, Breathe,
and Reclaim the Moment

The 3-3-3 Reset

What it's for: Racing thoughts, panic, emotional overload

Do it when: You feel like your mind is spiraling and you can't think straight

How it works:
Stop. Look around. Name out loud:

- 3 things you can see
- 3 things you can touch
- 3 slow, deep breaths

Why it helps:

This brings your brain out of the fog and back into the room with you. Simple sensory input helps calm your nervous system and interrupts anxious thinking.

Hand on Heart Check-In

What it's for: Feeling overwhelmed, invisible, unsafe, or alone

Do it when: You need comfort but can't find the words

How it works:
Place your hand on your chest. Close your eyes if you can. Say (out loud or in your head):

"I am here. I am safe. I am allowed to feel this."
"I've made it through hard things before. I'm still here."

Why it helps:
Physical touch releases oxytocin, a calming hormone. Hearing your own voice—especially speaking kindness—can trigger self-soothing.

The Five-Second Window

What it's for: Emotional reactivity, impulsive decisions, flash anger

Do it when: You're about to say something you'll regret or react from fear

How it works:

When you feel the urge to lash out or shut down, pause. Count to five. Just five seconds. Then ask:

"What do I need right now—not forever, just right now?"

Why it helps:

That short window lets your thinking brain catch up with your feeling brain. It gives you a moment to choose your next step instead of reacting.

The Safety Scan

What it's for: Hypervigilance, trauma triggers, body tension
Do it when: You know you're technically safe, but your body feels like you're in danger

How it works:
Look around the room. Say (or think):

"There's no threat here. I am safe in this room. The danger is not here."
Then name three things that confirm this:

- A locked door
- A calm face nearby
- Your own feet flat on the floor

Why it helps:
Trauma lives in the body. Logic doesn't override fear, but proof of safety in the present moment helps calm your system over time.

The Pocket Anchor

What it's for: Staying grounded during anxiety, panic, or grief

Do it when: You're out in public and need to feel tethered to something real

How it works:

Keep a small object with you: a coin, stone, piece of jewelry, rubber band, or prayer cloth. When things feel too much, grip it. Rub it between your fingers. Tell yourself:

"I'm holding this, so I don't have to hold everything else."

"This is my reminder that I'm still here."

Why it helps:

Physical anchors create a mental pause. They symbolize control and connection in a moment that feels out of control.

The Grounding Walk

What it's for: Disconnection, mental fog, depressive freeze

Do it when: You feel like you're "not here" or can't focus

How it works:
Go for a short walk—around your home, block, or hallway. With each step, say:

"This is my left foot. This is my right foot."
"I am here. I am moving. I am real."

Why it helps:
Movement engages both sides of your brain and helps regulate your nervous system. Naming your steps reconnects you to your body.

Name the Feeling, Don't Be the Feeling

What it's for: Emotional overwhelm, shame spirals, self-doubt

Do it when: You feel consumed by emotion

How it works:

Say out loud:

"I am feeling ___. But I am not ___."

Examples:

"I am feeling hopeless. But I am not hopeless."

"I am feeling afraid. But I am not fear."

Why it helps:

This separates who you are from what you're experiencing. You get to feel it without becoming it.

Call Yourself Back

What it's for: Worry, regret, past trauma, future fear
Do it when: You feel stuck in a memory or spiraling about what's next

How it works:
Sit still. Touch something real—your hands, your chair, your heart. Say:
"I don't live there anymore."
"I am allowed to be here now."

Why it helps:
Reminds your body and mind that the present moment is a safe place to land.

Breathe Like You Mean It

What it's for: Shallow breathing, anxiety, physical tension

Do it when: You feel like you can't catch your breath or the world is too loud

How it works:

Inhale slowly for 4 counts

Hold for 2 counts

Exhale for 6 counts
Repeat at least 3 times

Why it helps:

Regulates your nervous system and brings oxygen to your brain. A slower exhale tells your body: *We're not in danger in this momen*t.

Close the Loop

What it's for: Emotional buildup, long days, burnout
Do it when: You've been holding it together all day and need to let it go

How it works:
Stand up. Shake out your hands. Stretch your arms. Breathe deep. Say:

"This moment is finished. I don't have to carry it anymore."

Why it helps:
Stress is a cycle; this helps your body complete it. Even if nothing around you changes, you've signaled that *you* can move forward.

A Letter From Me to You

—from one dreamer to another

Hi friend,

If you made it to this part of the book, I just want to say thank you. Not just for reading, but for *staying*. For staying with your story even when it's hard. For staying with the belief (no matter how small) that there is still something good waiting for you, even in the middle of all this.

I wrote this book as a kind of love letter. The kind you keep with you and read in stolen moments, like while you wait to be seen by the dentist. The kind you pull out on a tough day when you need to remember who you are. And the kind you pull out to read on a good day when you want to be thankful for having made it to this day.

I'm not writing to you as someone who figured everything out. Because I haven't done that. I'm writing as someone who has faced her own darkness, her own breakdowns, her own "what's the point" kind of days. I've felt hopeless. I've felt numb. I've struggled to get out of bed. I've looked around at the world and wondered how we're supposed to survive this and still care about anything.

I've lived through enough to know that hope is real—and I've learned that it doesn't come all at once. It comes in little flickers. Quiet mornings. A deep breath. A glass of water. A peeled orange. A beautiful poem. One next right step. It comes through dreams, new friends and new experiences.

Some days, my hoping skill is strong. Other days, I have to dig for it. But I always come back to it, and it always brings me back to me.

If I could reach through these pages and sit beside you, I would tell you this: You are not broken. You are not behind. You are not too much or not enough. You are not all the lies we are routinely told. You are in the middle of something hard *and you are still here*. That alone is proof of your strength.

Please don't wait until life feels easier to start loving it again. Don't wait until the world is healed to believe that you deserve healing too. You don't have to fix everything before you get to rest, to hope, to begin again… to *dream*.

Start now. Start where you are.
Start *In the Meantime*.

With you always,
Deedee

Don't Stop Here.

Download your free *In the Meantime* Companion Toolkit

You've made it this far in the book—
which means you're still reaching for hope,
even when it feels far away.

I created the *In the Meantime Toolkit* to give you more than words on a page. Real tools you can use on your hardest days, in your quietest moments, or when you just need to remember that you're not alone.

Inside the Toolkit, You'll Find:

- Printable mental health grounding exercises
- The full Book Club Guide
- The full 21-day set of Journaling Prompts
- A Hope Playlist to carry you through
- And extras I only share with my readers—gentle, soulful reminders that this life still belongs *to you*.

Download your free *In the Meantime* companion toolkit here:

https://www.makeawaymedia.com/in-the-meantime/

… or scan the QR code.

This is more than a book.

This is a journey.

And you don't have to walk it alone.

With all my hope,

Deedee

About the Author

Deedee Cummings is a professional dreamer, author, therapist, and attorney from Louisville, Kentucky. She founded Make A Way Media to create diverse, hope-filled stories for children and adults, and is also the founder of the nonprofit It Pays to Read and the Louisville Book Festival. Her work—centered on healing, literacy, and the power of starting over—has been featured in Forbes, Essence, USA Today, and NPR. Cummings was appointed twice to Kentucky's Early Childhood Advisory Council by Governor Andy Beshear of Kentucky and continues to write and speak about the power of hope.

Are you ready to dream?

We can do it together.

Download your first chapter of How to Dream by Deedee Cummings here for free:

"This book is your guide to reclaiming the power of your dreams."

~Emely Rumble, LCSW
Author of Bibliotherapy in the Bronx and Founder of Literapy NYC